Modern Chinese (BOOK 2)
– Learn Chinese in a Simple and Successful Way
– Series 1, 2, 3, 4

by Vivienne Zhang

Copyright © 2012 Vivienne Zhang

All rights reserved.

ISBN: 1490388419
ISBN-13: 978-1490388410

Acknowledgements

There are many people without whose helpful support and encouragement BOOK 1, 2, 3, 4 would not have become a reality. I would like to express my heartfelt gratitude to my good friend, Pax Webb, for his patience and meticulous care in proofreading the drafts and offering suggestions.

I wish to thank my parents for their undivided support and interest, whose wisdom inspired me and encouraged me to go my own way, without whom I would be unable to complete these books. I am also very grateful to my siblings, especially my younger sister Vicky who shares my daily happiness and woes. My appreciation of their love for me truly goes beyond mere words.

I also give my sincere appreciation to all the teachers who have taught and encouraged me during my life studies. From their instructive courses and stimulating discussions I have acquired many insights and a genuine love for languages and linguistics.

I hope you find these books as interesting, challenging and rewarding as I did writing them.

Preface

In recent years, China has grown to be a powerhouse in the world economy. Mandarin, Putonghua in Chinese, has always been the world's most spoken language by sheer volume of native speakers but its value has also become especially important among foreigners and business professionals. With the ever increasing focus on international trade with China, Western interest in learning Chinese has grown exponentially.

As a Chinese native speaker fluent in English, I have been translating, interpreting and teaching for many years. I have not always been satisfied with the available books and materials for teaching Chinese to foreigners. Over the last several years I have tried, tested and perfected various lessons and techniques that apply well to Chinese studies. I have collected and now publish all of these modern techniques into books.

One of the unique features in these books is the literal translation into English of common Chinese expressions and vocabulary. For example, you can often see "lit." with the grammar points in BOOK 1, showing the direct translation of the Chinese text. This will reinforce an understanding of sentence structure and grammar which has proven to be instrumental in helping you retain the Chinese you have already learned. Other Chinese language books do not use this approach.

In BOOK 2, Part 1 provides more grammar points which continue from BOOK 1. There are useful examples to help you grasp each of the grammar points. Part 1 is arranged in such a way that any topic in this part can be studied independently.

Upon completion of this book, you will attain not only mastery of Chinese grammar and vocabulary, but also an expanded knowledge of Chinese writing.

Table of Contents

Part 1   **Grammar Points** 7

    Auxiliary Verbs 8

    Verbs and Tenses 20

    Common Verbs and Their Usages 37

    Adverbs 118

    Interjections 166

Part 2   **Appendix** 173

    Common Measure Words 174

    Common Words and Phrases 191

    Primer on Writing Chinese Characters 199

Part 1   Grammar Points

Auxiliary Verbs

1.

Can: huì 会 / **néng** 能 / **kěyǐ** 可以

(1) "huì" (can) expresses an innate ability or ability based on learning and knowledge. The negative pattern is "bú huì" (cannot/can't).

tāmen huì shuō zhōngwén.

他们会说中文。

They can speak Chinese.

tā bú huì xiě nà ge zì.

他不会写那个字。

He can't write that character.

(2) "néng" (can) expresses the physical ability or the unobstructed

ability to perform a certain/some action. "bù néng" (cannot/can't) is used when the performance is obstructed.

nǐ néng bǎ bīngxiāng bān dào nàbiān qù ma?

你能把冰箱搬到那边去吗?

Can you move the fridge over there?

(lit. You can bǎ fridge move to there go?)

(refer to BOOK 1 "Prepositions" 1, bǎ 把)

tā de hóulóng tòng, bù néng shuōhuà.

她的喉咙痛，不能说话。

Her throat is sore. She can't speak.

(lit. Her throat hurts/pain, can't speak.)

xiànzài zài xiū lù. wǒmen bù néng guò.

现在在修路。我们不能过。

The road is being repaired now. We can't cross it.

(lit. Now is repairing road. We can't cross.)

(3) "kěyǐ" (can) is sometimes used to express knowledge-based or physical ability. In this case, it's equal to "huì" and "néng". The negative is "bù kěyǐ" (cannot/can't).

nǐ kěyǐ xiě nǐ de zhōngwén míngzì ma?

你可以写你的中文名字吗？ (= huì 会)

Can you write your Chinese name?

(lit. You can write your Chinese name?)

tā yǐjīng qīshí suì le, dànshì tā hái kěyǐ qí zìxíngchē.

她已经七十岁了，但是她还可以骑自行车。(= néng 能)

She is already 70 years old, but can still ride a bike.

(lit. She already 70 years old, but she still can ride bike.)

(4) The primary use of "kěyǐ" (can) is to express the permission to perform an action. "bù kěyǐ" (cannot/can't) is used when the action is not allowed.

nǐ bù kěyǐ zài zhèlǐ chōuyān.

你不可以在这里抽烟。

You can't smoke here.

(lit. You can't here smoke.)

tā zhǐyǒu shíliù suì. bù kěyǐ hē jiǔ.

他只有十六岁。不可以喝酒。

He is only 16 years old. He cannot drink alcohol.

(lit. He only 16 years old. Can't drink alcohol.)

2.

Be able to: nénggòu 能够

"nénggòu" (be able to) expresses someone has the necessary power, resources, skills, time, opportunities, qualifications, etc, to do something.

wǒ bù nénggòu kāi zhè ge píngzi.

我不能够开这个瓶子。

I am not able to open this bottle.

tā nénggòu xiě yīnyuè.

她能够写音乐。

She is able to write music.

tāmen nénggòu tóupiào.

他们能够投票。

They are able to vote.

jīntiān tā nénggòu yóuyǒng.

今天 他 能够 游泳。

He is able to swim today.

(lit. Today he is able to swim.)

3.

May/Might: kěnéng 可能

Maybe/Perhaps/Probably (adverbs): kěnéng 可能 / yěxǔ 也许

míngtiān kěnéng huì xiàyǔ.

明天 可能 会 下雨。

It may rain tomorrow.

(lit. Tomorrow may will rain.)

tāmen kěnéng yǐjīng zài huǒchē zhàn le.

他们可能已经在火车站了。

They might already be at the train station.

fēijī wǎndiǎn le. wǒmen kěnéng huì chídào.

飞机晚点了。我们可能会迟到。

The plane is delayed. We will probably be late.

kěnéng tā qù kāihuì le.

可能他去开会了。

Maybe he went to have a meeting.

kěnéng / yěxǔ huì xiàyǔ.

可能 / 也许会下雨。

Perhaps it will rain.

4.

Should: yīnggāi 应该

Have to: bùdébù 不得不 / **děi** 得 **(objective)**

Must: bìxū 必须 / **kěndìng** 肯定 **(subjective)**

Certainly/Definitely/For sure (adverbs): yídìng 一定

tiānqì lěng. nǐ yīnggāi chuān duō yìdiǎn yīfú.

天气 冷。你 应该 穿 多 一点 衣服。

It's cold. You should wear more clothes.

(lit. Weather cold. You should wear many a little clothes.)

nǐ yīnggāi zǎo yìdian shuìjiào.

你 应该 早 一点 睡觉。

You should go to sleep a little earlier.

(lit. You should early a little sleep.)

jīntiān tā bùdébù xiě wán zhè fèn bàogào.

今天他不得不写完这份报告。

He has to finish writing this report today.

(lit. Today he has to write finished this report.)

nǐ děi zǒu kuài diǎn cái néng gǎnshàng tāmen.

你得走快点才能赶上他们。

You have to walk fast to catch up with them.

(lit. You have to walk fast little only just can catch up them.)

rúguǒ wǒmen xiǎng zhǔnshí dàodá, wǒmen bìxū gǎnkuài.

如果我们想准时到达，我们必须赶快。

If we want to arrive on time, we must hurry.

(lit. If we want on time arrive, we must hurry.)

tā kěndìng shì lèi le.

她 肯 定 是 累 了。

She must be tired.

tā yídìng huì mǎi nà liàng chē.

他 一 定 会 买 那 辆 车。

He will certainly buy that car.

(lit. He certainly will buy that car.)

wǒ bù yídìng qù.

我 不 一 定 去。

I am not definitely going. (I may not go.)

(lit. I not definitely go.)

5.

Would like: xiǎngyào 想要

Would rather: nìngyuàn 宁愿

Be willing (adjective): yuànyì 愿意

wǒ xiǎngyào hé nǐ yìqǐ qù pǎobù.

我 想要 和 你 一起 去 跑步。

I would like to go running together with you.

(lit. I would like with you together go running.)

tā nìngyuàn qù jiànshēnfáng.

他 宁愿 去 健身房。

He would rather go to the gym.

nǐ yuànyì bāng wǒ jiějué zhè ge wèntí ma?

你愿意帮我解决这个问题吗?

Are you willing to help me solve this problem?

(lit. You willing help me solve this problem?)

wǒ yuànyì gēn nǐ hézuò.

我愿意跟你合作。

I am willing to cooperate with you.

(lit. I willing with you cooperate.)

Verbs and Tenses

A Chinese verb does not change its form with tense or subject. The basic Chinese sentence order is "Subject + Predicate (verb) + Object (noun), the same as English.

wǒ xuéxí zhōngwén.

我 学习 中文。

I learn Chinese.

tā xuéxí zhōngwén.

他 学习 中文.

He learns Chinese.

qùnián tāmen xuéxí zhōngwén.

去年 他们 学习 中文。

Last year they learnt Chinese.

Two or three verbs used together (to express a goal):

wǒmen huì lái kàn nǐ.

我们会来看你。

We will come to see you.

wǒ xiǎng hē yì bēi kāfēi.

我想喝一杯咖啡。

I want to drink a cup of coffee.

(the difference between "xiǎng" (want to do something) and "yào" (want something), refer to "Common Verbs and Their Usages" 7 in this book)

wǒ xiǎng qù kàn wǒ de fùmǔ.

我 想 去 看 我 的 父母。

I want to go to visit/see my parents.

tāmen xǐhuān qù yóuyǒng.

他们 喜欢 去 游泳。

They like to go swimming.

1.

Past tense of verbs: dòngcí guòqù shí 动词过去时

In Chinese, using time words such as "yesterday", "last month", "two years ago" is the simplest way to indicate past tense.

zuótiān shì tā de shēngrì.

昨天 是 她 的 生日。

Yesterday was her birthday.

shàng ge yuè tā kāishǐ gōngzuò.

上个月他开始工作。

He started to work last month.

(lit. Last month he started work.)

liǎng nián qián wǒmen qù zhōngguó lǚyóu.

两年前我们去中国旅游。

We travelled to China two years ago.

(lit. Two years ago we went China travel.)

2.

Verbs with "le": dòngcí jiā "le" de yòngfǎ 动词加"了"的用法

(1) "le" is placed after the verb of a sentence or at the end of the sentence, following the object. It is used to indicate the past action or implies that something is no longer in the same state as it was.

wǒ chī le liǎng kuài dàngāo.

我 吃 了 两 块 蛋糕。

I ate two pieces of cake.

tāmen lái zhōngguó le.

他们 来 中国 了。

They came to China.

jīntiān shàngwǔ tā qù le gōngsī.

今天 上午 他 去 了 公司。

He went to the company this morning.

(lit. Today morning he went company.)

tā bú shì yīshēng le.

他 不 是 医生 了。

He is no longer a doctor.

(lit. He not is doctor.)

(2) If "le" is placed at the end of the sentence, following an adjective or adverb, it emphasizes the completion of an action or a state.

tā bìng le.

她 病 了。

She is sick.

tā xiànzài hǎo duō le.

她 现在 好 多 了。

She is much better now.

(lit. She now good many.)

tāmen lái zǎo le.

他们 来 早 了。

They came early.

jīntiān tā qǐchuáng wǎn le.

今天 她 起床 晚 了。

She got up late today.

(lit. Today she got up late.)

3.

Be doing: zài 在 / zhèngzài 正在

(1) In Chinese, "zài" precedes a verb to indicate the continuous tense. It conveys the idea that the action is/was underway.

tāmen zài gōngzuò.

他们 在 工作。

They are working.

tā zài zuò fàn.

他 在 做 饭。

He is cooking.

jīntiān xiàwǔ wǒ zài zhǎo wǒ de gǒu.

今天 下午 我 在 找 我 的 狗。

I was looking for my dog this afternoon.

(lit. Today afternoon I was looking for my dog.)

(2) "zhèngzài" precedes a verb to indicate that an action is happening right now.

tāmen zhèngzài biǎoyǎn wǔdǎo.

他们 正在 表演 舞蹈。

They are performing a dance.

wǒmen zhèngzài shàngkè.

我们 正在 上课。

We are having a class.

tā zhèngzài kàn diànshì.

他 正在 看 电视。

He is watching TV.

4.

Have been doing: yìzhí zài 一直在

zhèxiē tiān yìzhí zài xiàyǔ.

这些天一直在下雨。

It has been raining these days.

(lit. These days have been raining.)

tāmen yìzhí zài děng nǐ.

他们一直在等你。

They have been waiting for you.

tā yìzhí zài zhè ge gōngsī gōngzuò.

他一直在这个公司工作。

He has been working in this company.

(lit. He has been in this company working.)

5.

Verbs with "guò": dòngcí jiā "guò" de yòngfǎ 动词加"过"的用法

"guò" is equal to the English expressions "have been" or "have done". It follows a verb to indicate the unspecified past experience. "méiyǒu" (have not / has not) should be placed before a verb.

wǒ qù guò nà ge chēzhàn.

我去过那个车站。

I have been to that station.

wǒ kàn guò jīntiān de bàozhǐ.

我看过今天的报纸。

I have read today's newspaper.

tā méiyǒu kàn guò zhè běn shū.

她没有看过这本书。

She has not read this book.

tāmen méiyǒu zuò guò fēijī.

他们没有坐过飞机。

They have not taken a plane.

6.

Future tense: jiānglái shí 将来时 (the most common 3 ways)

(1) To use time words such as "tomorrow" and "next month" to express future tense.

míngtiān tā qù běijīng.

明天 他 去 北京。

He is going to Beijing tomorrow.

(lit. Tomorrow he goes Beijing.)

xià ge zhōumò tāmen lái kàn wǒ.

下 个 周末 他们 来 看 我。

They are coming to visit/see me next weekend.

(lit. Next weekend they come see me.)

(2) To use "huì" (will) and "yào" (be going to) to express future tense. "huì" here doesn't mean "can" and "yào" doesn't mean "to want".

tā huì lái xiūlǐ kōngtiáo.

他 会 来 修理 空调。

He will come to repair the air-conditioning.

sījī huì qù jiē nǐ.

司机 会 去 接 你。

The driver will go to pick you up.

xià ge xīngqī wǒ yào qù shànghǎi.

下 个 星期 我 要 去 上海。

I am going to Shanghai next week.

(lit. Next week I am going Shanghai.)

míngtiān shàngwǔ wǒmen yào kāihuì.

明天 上午 我们 要 开会。

We are going to / will have a meeting tomorrow morning.

(lit. Tomorrow morning we are going to have a meeting.)

(To avoid the misunderstanding of "huì" (will) and "huì" in "kāihuì" (have a meeting), because both "huì" have the same pronunciation and Chinese character, we use "yào" instead.)

(3) "jiù" implies that something is going to happen very soon. It's often used together with "mǎshàng *(lit. horse above)*" (right now).

wǒmen mǎshàng jiù dào.

我们 马上 就 到。

= wǒmen hěn kuài jiù dào.

= 我们 很 快 就 到。

We will arrive very soon.

(lit. We horse above jiù arrive. = We very soon jiù arrive.)

míngtiān wǒ jiù huán gěi nǐ.

明天 我 就 还 给 你。

I will give it back to you tomorrow.

(lit. Tomorrow I jiù give back to you.)

xià ge xīngqī wǒ jiù yào líkāi zhè ge chéngshì.

下 个 星期 我 就 要 离开 这 个 城市。

I am leaving this city next week.

(lit. Next week I jiù am going to leave this city.)

7.

Verbs with "dào": dòngcí jiā "dào" de yòngfǎ 动词加"到"的用法

"dào" follows certain verbs such as hear, see, meet, and find, to emphasize the successful result of an action.

nǐ tīngdào tā zài tán gāngqín le ma?

你 听到 她 在 弹钢琴 了 吗?

Did you hear that she was playing piano?

(lit. You heard she was playing piano?)

wǒ méiyǒu kàndào nǐ de yǎnjìng.

我 没有 看到 你 的 眼镜。

I didn't see your glasses.

wǒmen zài shèngdànjié pàiduì shàng kàndào hěnduō péngyǒu.

我们 在 圣诞节 派对 上 看到 很多 朋友。

We met many friends at the Christmas party.

(lit. We at the Christmas party up met many friends.)

wǒ zhǎodào le yì běn shū, shì gěi nǐ de.

我找到了一本书，是给你的。

I found a book for you.

(lit. I found a book, is for you.)

Common Verbs and Their Usages

1.

To be: shì 是, To be not: bú shì 不是

nǐ shì lǎoshī ma?

你 是 老师 吗?

Are you a teacher?

(lit. You are teacher?)

shì de, wǒ shì.

是 的, 我 是。

Yes, I am.

bù, wǒ bú shì.

不，我不是。

No, I am not.

(lit. No, I not am.)

tāmen shì wǒ de tóngshì.

他们是我的同事。

They are my colleagues.

zhè bú shì wǒ de shū.

这不是我的书。

This is not my book.

(lit. This not is my book.)

2.

(1) When "shì" (to be) is used with a noun, the noun can be modified by a pronoun or an adjective.

wǒ shì yīshēng.

我 是 医生。

I am a doctor.

tā shì wǒ de péngyǒu.

她 是 我 的 朋友。

She is my friend.

(2) "shì" (to be) can be omitted when used with an adjective. The adjective can be modified by an adverb.

wǒ è le.

我 饿 了。

I am hungry.

(lit. I hungry.)

tā hěn cōngmíng.

他 很 聪明。

He is intelligent/smart.

(lit. He very intelligent/smart.)

wǒ bù shūfú.

我 不 舒服。

I am not comfortable. (sick)

(lit. I not comfortable.)

3.

Negative form of verbs 动词否定式

(1) bù 不

To indicate that an action does not occur or will not occur (don't/doesn't, won't; in both present and future tenses), "bù" is put before a verb to express the negation.

tā bù xǐhuān hē chá.

他不喜欢喝茶。

He doesn't like to drink tea.

tā bú zài zhèlǐ gōngzuò.

她不在这里工作。

She doesn't work here.

(lit. She doesn't here work.)

tāmen bú qù pǎobù.

他们不去跑步。

They won't go running.

(2) méiyǒu 没有

To indicate that an action did not occur or has not occurred (didn't, haven't/hasn't; in both past and present perfect tenses), "méi(yǒu)" precedes a verb to express the negation.

jīntiān shàngwǔ tā méiyǒu qù shàngbān.

今天 上午 她 没有 去 上班。

She didn't go to work this morning.

(lit. Today morning she didn't go to work.)

wǒ méi(yǒu) chī zǎofàn.

我 没(有) 吃 早饭。

I did not eat breakfast.

zhè ge yuè wǒ méiyǒu kàn diànyǐng.

这 个 月 我 没有 看 电影。

This month I haven't seen a movie.

Exceptions:

yǐqián wǒ bù zhīdào.

以前 我 不 知道。

I didn't know before.

(lit. Before I not know.)

(There is "yǐqián" (before) to imply that it's past tense, so there's no need to have "le" in the sentence.)

yǐqián wǒ bú rènshí tāmen.

以前 我 不 认识 他们。

I didn't know them before.

(lit. Before I not know them.)

dāngshí wǒ bù dǒng wèishéme nǐ huàn le gōngzuò.

当时 我 不 懂 为什么 你 换 了 工作。

= dāngshí wǒ bù míngbái wèishéme nǐ huàn le gōngzuò.

= 当时 我 不 明白 为什么 你 换 了 工作。

I didn't understand at that time why you changed your job.

(lit. At that time I not understand why you changed job.)

(There is "dāngshí" (at that time) to imply that it's past tense.)

(3) Don't: bié 别 / bú yào 不要

bié wàngjì chī yào, yì tiān sān cì.

别 忘记 吃 药，一 天 三 次。

Don't forget to take the medicine three times a day.

(lit. Don't forget eat medicine, one day three times.)

bié dānxīn.

别 担心。

Don't worry.

bié jǐnzhāng.

别 紧张。

Don't be nervous.

bú yào shēngqì.

不 要 生气。

Don't be angry.

bú yào làngfèi shíwù.

不 要 浪费 食物。

Don't waste food.

(4) Never: cóng(lái) bù 从(来)不

"cóng(lái) bù" (never) precedes the verb to express that something never happens.

tāmen cóng(lái) bù chōuyān.

他们 从(来) 不 抽烟。

They never smoke.

tā cóng(lái) bú zuò díshì qù shàngbān.

他 从(来) 不 坐 的 士 去 上班。

He never takes a taxi to work.

(lit. He never sits taxi go/to work.)

xīngqī tiān tā cóng(lái) bù kāichē.

星期 天 她 从(来) 不 开车。

She never drives her car on Sundays.

(lit. Sundays she never drives car.)

(5) Have never: cóng(lái) méi(yǒu) 从(来)没(有)

When "cóng(lái) méi(yǒu)" (have never) precedes the verb to express that something has never happened, "guò" should be placed after the verb.

Patten: S + 从(来)没(有)(cóng(lái) méi(yǒu)) + V. + 过(guò) + O

tāmen cóng(lái) méi(yǒu) qù guò nà ge chéngshì.

他们 从(来) 没(有) 去 过 那 个 城市。

They have never been to that city.

wǒ cóng(lái) méi(yǒu) jiàn guò tāmen.

我 从(来) 没(有) 见 过 他们。

I have never seen them.

tāmen cóng(lái) méi(yǒu) chī guò zhōngguó cài.

他们 从(来) 没(有) 吃过 中国 菜。

They have never had/eaten Chinese food.

tā cóng(lái) méi(yǒu) zuò guò fàn.

她 从(来) 没(有) 做 过 饭。

She has never cooked.

wǒ cóng(lái) méi(yǒu) chōu guò yān.

我 从(来) 没(有) 抽 过 烟。

I have never smoked.

4.

Have/Has: yǒu 有

Don't/Doesn't have: méiyǒu 没有

There is/are/was/were: yǒu 有

There isn't/aren't/wasn't/weren't: méiyǒu 没有

Didn't (do something) / Haven't/Hasn't (done something): méiyǒu 没有 **(refer to "Common Verbs and Their Usages" 3 (2) in this book)**

tāmen yǒu yí ge dà de bàngōngshì.

他们有一个大的办公室。

They have a big office.

jīntiān wǒ méiyǒu shíjiān kàn diànshì.

今天我没有时间看电视。

I don't have time to watch TV today.

(lit. Today I don't have time watch TV.)

fángzi hòumiàn yǒu yí ge wǎngqiú chǎng.

房子 后面 有 一个 网球 场。

There is a tennis court behind the house.

(lit. House behind has a tennis court.)

fùjìn méiyǒu dìtiě zhàn.

附近 没有 地铁 站。

There are no subway stations nearby.

(lit. Nearby don't have subway stations.)

5.

Know (people, also Chinese characters and location): rènshí 认识

Know (things): zhīdào 知道

Recognize: rènchū 认出

Can't/Couldn't recognize: rèn bù chū 认不出

nǐ rènshí zhèlǐ de qítā wàiguórén ma?

你 认识 这里 的 其他 外国人 吗?

Do you know other foreigners here?

(lit. You know here's other foreigners?)

nǐ rènshí zhōngguó hànzì ma?

你 认识 中国 汉字 吗?

Do you know Chinese characters?

(lit. You know Chinese characters?)

wǒ rènshí zhōngguó hànzì, kěshì wǒ bù zhīdào zěnme xiě.

我 认识 中国 汉字, 可是 我 不 知道 怎么 写。

I know Chinese characters, but I don't know how to write them.

(lit. I know Chinese characters, but I don't know how write.)

duìbùqǐ, wǒ bú rènshí lù.

对不起，我不认识路。

Sorry, I don't know the way.

(lit. Sorry, I don't know road.)

tā zhīdào tā huì bèi pài qù zhōngguó gōngzuò.

他知道他会被派去中国工作。

He knows he will be sent to work in China.

(lit. He knows he will be sent go/to China work.)

zuótiān wǎnshàng zài pàiduì shàng, wǒ méiyǒu rènchū nǐ.

昨天晚上在派对上，我没有认出你。

I didn't recognize you last night at the party.

(lit. Yesterday night at the party up, I didn't recognize you.)

nǐ biàn le hěnduō. wǒ chàdiǎn rèn bù chū nǐ.

你变了很多。我差点认不出你。

You have changed a lot. I nearly couldn't recognize you.

6.

Help (verb/noun): bāng(zhù) 帮(助)/bāngmáng 帮忙

Do…a favor: bāng…yí ge máng 帮…一个忙

wǒ xiǎngyào bāng(zhù) nǐ.

我 想要 帮(助) 你。

I'd like to help you.

tā xūyào nǐ de bāngzhù/bāngmáng.

她需要你的 帮助/帮忙。

She needs your help.

nǐ kěyǐ bāng wǒ yí ge máng ma?

你 可以 帮 我 一个 忙 吗?

Can you do me a favor?

(lit. You can help/do me a favor?)

7.

Want: yào 要 (want something); xiǎng 想 (want to do something)

Think: xiǎng 想 / juéde 觉得 / rènwéi 认为

Presume/Thought: yǐwéi 以为

Miss: xiǎng 想

Need: xūyào 需要

Don't need: bù xūyào 不需要 / bú yòng 不用

wǒ yào yì bēi chá.

我要一杯茶。

I want a cup of tea.

wǒ xiǎng hē yì bēi chá.

我想喝一杯茶。

I want to drink a cup of tea.

wǒ xiǎng/juéde/rènwéi zhè shì yí ge hǎo zhǔyì.

我想/觉得/认为这是一个好主意。

I think this is a good idea.

wǒ yǐwéi zuótiān huì xiàyǔ.

我以为昨天会下雨。

I thought it would rain yesterday (but it didn't).

(lit. I thought yesterday would rain.)

wǒ yǐwéi nǐ shì rìběnrén.

我 以为 你 是 日本人。

I thought you were Japanese, (but you are Korean).

wǒ xiǎng nǐ.

我 想 你。

I miss you.

wǒ xūyào qù mǎi yìxiē shèngdànjié lǐwù.

我 需要 去 买 一些 圣诞节 礼物。

I need to go to buy some Christmas gifts.

wǒ míngtiān bù xūyào / bú yòng qù shàngbān.

我明天不需要/不用去上班。

I don't need to go to work tomorrow.

(lit. I tomorrow don't need go to work.)

8.

Go: qù 去 / zǒu 走

Will go to: huì qù 会去

Walk: zǒulù 走路

To: qù 去 / dào 到

Come back/Return: huílái 回来 *(lit. back come)*

wǒmen yìqǐ qù kàn diànyǐng.

我们一起去看电影。

Let's go to watch a movie together.

(lit. We together go watch movie.)

wǒmen zǒu ba.

我们 走 吧。

Let's go.

(lit. We go.)

tā huì qù běijīng chūchāi.

他 会 去 北京 出差。

He will go to Beijing for a business trip.

(lit. He will go Beijing business trip.)

wǒ zài zǒulù qù/dào shāngdiàn.

我 在 走路 去/到 商店。

I am walking to the shop.

èrlínglíngjiǔ nián wǒ huílái le zhōngguó.

二零零九年我回来了中国。

I came back / returned to China in 2009.

(lit. 2009 year I back came China.)

Common phrases with "qù" (go) and "lái" (come):

go out: chūqù 出去

come out: chūlái 出来

go back: huíqù 回去

come back: huílái 回来

go in / enter: jìnqù 进去

come in: jìnlái 进来

go over: guòqù 过去

come over: guòlái 过来

9.

Leave: líkāi 离开 / **zǒu** 走

Leave (put/forget)…in/on/at…: fàng/wàng…zài… 放/忘…在…

Arrive in/at: dào(dá) 到(达)

tā wǔ suì de shíhòu líkāi le xiānggǎng.

他 五 岁 的 时候 离开 了 香港。

He left Hong Kong when he was five years old.

(lit. He five years old when left Hong Kong.)

bàn ge xiǎoshí qián tāmen líkāi / zǒu le.

半 个 小时 前 他们 离开 / 走 了。

They left half an hour ago.

(lit. Half an hour ago they left.)

wǒ kěyǐ bǎ wǒ de xínglǐ fàng zài nǐ jiā ma?

我可以把我的行李放在你家吗?

simpler way: wǒ kěyǐ fàng wǒ de xínglǐ zài nǐ jiā ma?

simpler way: 我可以放我的行李在你家吗?

Can I leave my luggage at your house?

(lit. I can bǎ my luggage put at your home?)

(simpler way: lit. I can put my luggage at your home?)

(refer to BOOK 1 "Prepositions" 1, bǎ 把)

wǒ bǎ shǒujī wàng zài jiā lǐ le.

我把手机忘在家里了。

I left my mobile phone at home.

(lit. I bǎ hand machine forgot at home in/inside.)

wǒmen liǎng ge xiǎoshí qián dàodá le fēijī chǎng.

我们 两 个 小时 前 到达 了 飞机 场。

We arrived at the airport two hours ago.

(lit. We two hours ago arrived airport.)

wǒmen yīnggāi shàngwǔ jiǔ diǎn yǐqián dào bàngōngshì.

我们 应该 上午 九 点 以前 到 办公室。

We should arrive at the office before 9a.m.

(lit. We should morning 9 o'clock before arrive office.)

10.

Do/Make: zuò 做

Common phrases with "zuò" (do/make):

do things/something (abstract): zuò shìqíng 做事情

do business: zuò shēngyì 做生意

do homework: zuò zuòyè 做作业

do housework: zuò jiāwù 做家务

make clothes: zuò yīfú 做衣服

make dumplings: zuò jiǎozi 做饺子

cook: zuò fàn 做饭 *(lit. make rice)*

tā zuò le shíwǔ nián de shēngyì.

他做了十五年的生意。

He has done business for 15 years.

(lit. He did 15 years' business.)

háizimen zài zuò zuòyè.

孩子们 在 做 作业。

The children are doing homework.

zhè ge cáiféng zuò de yīfú zhìliàng hěn hǎo.

这 个 裁缝 做 的 衣服 质量 很 好。

This tailor makes clothes with a high quality.

(lit. This tailor makes clothes quality very good.)

tāmen hěn shàncháng zuò jiǎozi.

他们 很 擅长 做 饺子。

They are very good at making dumplings.

Exceptions:

make money: zhuànqián/zhèngqián 赚钱/挣钱

make a mistake: fàn cuòwù 犯错误 *(lit. commit)*

make an excuse: zhǎo jièkǒu 找借口 *(lit. look for)*

tāmen gōngzuò hěnduō, dànshì zhuànqián/zhèngqián hěnshǎo.

他们 工作 很多，但是 赚钱/挣钱 很少。

They work a lot, but make very little money.

(lit. They work a lot, but make money very little.)

wǒmen bù yīnggāi fàn tóngyàng de cuòwù.

我们 不 应该 犯 同样 的 错误。

We should not make the same mistake.

(lit. We not should commit same mistake.)

zhǎo tài duō jièkǒu bù hǎo.

找 太 多 借口 不 好。

It's not good to make too many excuses.

(lit. Look for too many excuses not good.)

11.

Play: wán 玩

Good to play / Fun: hǎo wán 好玩

Play football: tī zúqiú 踢足球 *(lit. kick football)*

Play basketball: dǎ lánqiú 打篮球 *(lit. hit basketball)*

Play tennis: dǎ wǎngqiú 打网球 *(lit. hit tennis)*

Play guitar: tán jítā 弹吉他 *(lit. pluck guitar)*

Play piano: tán gāngqín 弹钢琴 *(lit. pluck piano)*

háizimen zài gōngyuán wán.

孩子们 在 公园 玩。

The children are playing in the park.

(lit. Children are in park playing.)

běijīng hǎo wán ma?

北京 好 玩 吗?

Was it fun in Beijing?

(lit. Beijing good play?)

tā xǐhuān tī zúqiú, dànshì bù xǐhuān dǎ lánqiú.

他 喜欢 踢 足球，但是 不 喜欢 打 篮球。

He likes to play football, but not basketball.

(lit. He likes kick football, but doesn't like hit basketball.)

tā yìbiān tán gāngqín yìbiān chànggē.

她 边 弹 钢琴 边 唱歌。

She is singing while playing piano.

(lit. She is plucking piano and singing.)

(refer to BOOK 1 "Conjunctions" 4, yìbiān…yìbiān…一边…一边…)

12.

Buy: mǎi 买

Sell: mài 卖

Thing(s)/Something/Stuff (visible): dōngxī 东西

Thing(s)/Something (invisible, abstract): shìqíng 事情

wǒ xiǎng mǎi yìxiē chéngzi.

我想买一些橙子。

I want to buy some oranges.

tāmen zài mài huā.

他们在卖花。

They are selling flowers.

wǒmen yào qù chāoshì mǎi dōngxī.

我们 要 去 超市 买 东西。

We are going to the supermarket to buy things.

(lit. We are going to go supermarket buy things.)

xiǎohái xiǎng chī dōngxī.

小孩 想 吃 东西。

The child wants to eat something.

jīntiān wǒ yǒu hěnduō shìqíng zuò.

今天 我 有 很多 事情 做。

I have lots of things to do today.

(lit. Today I have lots of things do.)

13.

Spend (money, time): huā 花

Flower: huā 花

tā huā le hěnduō qián mǎi yīfú.

她花了很多钱买衣服。

She spent a lot of money buying clothes.

tā měi tiān huā yí ge xiǎoshí kàn bàozhǐ.

他每天花一个小时看报纸。

He spends an hour reading newspaper every day.

(lit. He every day spends one hour look newspaper.)

zhèxiē huā fēicháng piàoliàng.

这些 花 非常 漂亮。

These flowers are extremely beautiful.

14.

Look for: zhǎo 找 (process)

Find: zhǎodào 找到 (successful result)

nǐ zài zhǎo shénme?

你 在 找 什么?

What are you looking for?

(lit. You are looking for what?)

tāmen zài zhǎo tāmen de gǒu.

他们 在 找 他们 的 狗。

They were looking for their dog.

jīntiān xiàwǔ tāmen zhǎodào le tāmen de gǒu.

今天 下午 他们 找到 了 他们 的 狗。

They found their dog this afternoon.

(lit. Today afternoon they found their dog.)

zài chē shàng, wǒ méiyǒu zhǎodào wǒ de shǒujī.

在 车 上，我 没有 找到 我 的 手机。

I didn't find my cell phone in the car.

(lit. In car up, I didn't find my hand machine.)

15.

(1) Common verbs with "jiàn" (to perceive; function: to indicate the successful result of an action): 见

to see: kànjiàn 看见

to hear: tīngjiàn 听见

(2) Common verbs with "dào" (to attain a goal, to acquire; function: to emphasize the successful result of an action): 到

to look –> to see/meet: kàndào 看到

to listen –> to hear: tīngdào 听到

to smell –> to have smelled: wéndào 闻到

to look for –> to find: zhǎodào 找到

to get –> to have got: dédào 得到

to receive –> to have received: shōudào 收到

to shop for –> to buy/purchase: mǎidào 买到

16.

See/Meet: jiàn 见 / jiànmiàn 见面

"jiànmiàn" (see/meet) is placed at the end of the sentence to express two or more than two people meeting each other.

míngtiān jiàn.

明天 见。

See you tomorrow

(lit. Tomorrow see.)

yí huì jiàn.

一会 见。

See you in a while.

(lit. A while see.)

xià ge xīngqī wǒ yào jiàn yí ge péngyǒu.

下 个 星期 我 要 见 一 个 朋友。

I am going to meet a friend next week.

(lit. Next week I am going to meet a friend.)

shàng ge xīngqī tā jiàn le tā māma.

上 个 星期 她 见 了 她 妈妈。

She met her mother last week.

(lit. Last week she met her mother.)

tāmen měi ge yuè jiànmiàn.

他们 每 个 月 见面。

They see each other every month.

(lit. They every month see.)

wǒmen zhè ge xīngqī liù jiànmiàn zěnmeyàng?

我们 这 个 星期 六 见面 怎么样?

What/How about meeting this Saturday?

(lit. We this Saturday meet what/how about?)

17.

See / Meet / Visit (informal) / Look / Watch / Read / Check (informal): kàn 看

Visit (formal): bàifǎng 拜访

Check (formal): jiǎnchá 检查

Show (somebody): gěi…kàn 给…看

wǒ qù kàn le yīshēng.

我 去 看 了 医生。

I went to see a doctor.

xià ge xīngqī wǒ qù kàn wǒ zuì hǎo de péngyǒu.

下个星期我去看我最好的朋友。

I am going to meet/visit my best friend next week.

(lit. Next week I go see my best friend.)

zuótiān wǒmen bàifǎng le wáng lǎoshī.

昨天我们拜访了王老师。

We visited teacher Wang yesterday.

(lit. Yesterday we visited Wang teacher.)

tāmen zhǐ shì kàn kàn. tāmen bú huì mǎi.

他们只是看看。他们不会买。

They are only looking. They won't buy.

(lit. They only are looking looking. They not will buy.)

tāmen zài kàn yí bù xīn de diànyǐng.

他们在看一部新的电影。

They are watching a new movie.

tā kàn guò hěnduō shū.

他看过很多书。

He has read many books.

nǐ kěyǐ bāng wǒ kànkàn wǒ de diànnǎo yǒu shéme wèntí ma?

你可以帮我看看我的电脑有什么问题吗?

Could you help me check what the problem is with my computer?

(lit. You can help me look look my computer has what problem?)

hǎiguān rényuán zài jiǎnchá tāmen de xínglǐ.

海关人员在检查他们的行李。

The customs officers are checking their luggage.

qǐng gěi tāmen kàn zhèxiē yàngpǐn.

请 给 他们 看 这些 样品。

Please show these samples to them.

(lit. Please to/give them look these samples.)

18.

It depends: kàn qíngkuàng 看情况 *(lit. look situation)*

Seem + adjective: kànshàngqù 看上去 *(lit. look up go)* / **hǎoxiàng** 好像

Seem + to have done: hǎoxiàng 好像

Look like: kànqǐlái xiàng 看起来像 *(lit. look up come like)* / **zhǎngde xiàng** 长得像 *(lit. grow like)*

kàn qíngkuàng. rúguǒ míngtiān bú xiàyǔ, wǒmen qù dǎ wǎngqiú.

看 情况。如果 明天 不 下雨，我们 去 打 网球。

It depends. We will go to play tennis if it doesn't rain tomorrow.

(lit. Look situation. If tomorrow doesn't rain, we go play tennis.)

tā kànshàngqù / hǎoxiàng hěn shāngxīn.

她 看上去 / 好像 很 伤心。

She seems very sad.

(lit. She look up go very sad.)

wǒ yǐqián hǎoxiàng jiàn guò tāmen.

我 以前 好像 见 过 他们。

I seem to have met them before.

(lit. I before seem have met them.)

tā kànqǐlái xiàng / zhǎngde xiàng wǒ de péngyǒu, lìlì.

她 看起来 像 / 长得 像 我 的 朋友，莉莉。

She looks like my friend, Lily.

(lit. She looks up come like / grows like my friend, Lily.)

19.

Listen to: tīng 听

Hear: tīngdào 听到

Hear of / Hear that…: tīng shuō 听说 *(lit. listen say)*

Sound like: tīngqǐlái xiàng 听起来像 *(lit. listen up come like)*

wǒ xǐhuān tīng zhè shǒu gē.

我 喜欢 听 这 首 歌。

I like listening to this song.

nǐ tīngdào nà shēngyīn le ma?

你听到那声音了吗?

Did you hear that sound?

(lit. You heard that sound?)

wǒ tīngshuō míngnián nǐ huì bān dào běijīng.

我听说明年你会搬到北京。

I heard that you would move to Beijing next year.

(lit. I listened say next year you would move to/arrive Beijing.)

tā tīng péngyǒu shuō běijīng kǎoyā hěn hǎochī.

他听朋友说北京烤鸭很好吃。

He heard from friends that Beijing roast duck is very delicious.

(lit. I listened friends say Beijing roast duck very good eat.)

tā de shēngyīn tīngqǐlái xiàng wǒ māma de.

她的声音听起来像我妈妈的。

Her voice sounds like my mother's.

(lit. Her voice listens up come like my mother's.)

20.

Say: shuō 说

Speak (languages): shuō 说

Speak: shuōhuà 说话 / jiǎnghuà 讲话

Talk: shuōhuà 说话 / tánhuà 谈话 (formal)

Chat: liáotiān 聊天

Discuss: shāngliáng 商量

tā shuō tā huì chídào shí fēnzhōng.

他说他会迟到十分钟。

He said he would be 10 minutes late.

(lit. He said he would late 10 mintues.)

tā huì shuō wǔ zhǒng yǔyán.

她会说五种语言。

She can speak five languages.

tāmen shuōhuà/jiǎnghuà tài dàshēng.

他们说话/讲话太大声。

They speak too loud.

tāmen zài hé kèhù tánhuà.

他们在和客户谈话。

They are talking with the clients.

(lit. They are with clients talking.)

hěnduō rén xǐhuān zài wǎngshàng liáotiān.

很多 人 喜欢 在 网上 聊天。

Many people like chatting online.

(lit. Many people like on net up chat.)

tāmen zài shāngliáng zěnmeyàng jiějué zhè ge wèntí.

他们 在 商量 怎么样 解决 这 个 问题。

They are discussing how to solve this problem.

21.

Open / Turn on : kāi 开

Close / Turn off: guān 关

Drive (a car): kāi chē 开车

Start: kāishǐ 开始

Have a meeting: kāihuì 开会

qǐng guān mén.

请关门。

Close the door, please.

(lit. Please close door.)

nǐ jièyì wǒ kāi chuāng ma?

你介意我开窗吗?

Do you mind if I open the window?

(lit. You mind I open window?)

tā wàng le guān diànshì.

她忘了关电视。

She forgot to turn off the TV.

(lit. She forgot turn off TV.)

yǒudiǎn àn. qǐng kāi dēng.

有点 暗。请 开 灯。

It's a bit dark. Please turn on the lights.

(lit. A little dark. Please turn on lights.)

tā shíbā suì kāishǐ kāichē.

他 十八 岁 开始 开车。

He started to drive at 18 years old.

(lit. He 18 years old started drive car.)

míngtiān wǒmen xūyào kāihuì.

明天 我们 需要 开会。

We need to have a meeting tomorrow.

(lit. Tomorrow we need have a meeting.)

22.

Put on / Wear: chuān 穿 / chuānshàng 穿上

Take off: tuō 脱 / tuōdiào 脱掉

wàimiàn hěn lěng. nǐ yīnggāi chuānshàng zhè jiàn dàyī.

外面 很 冷。你 应该 穿上 这 件 大衣。

It's cold outside. You should put on this coat.

(lit. Outside very cold. You should put on this coat.)

wǒ bù xǐhuān chuān zhè jiàn wàitào.

我 不 喜欢 穿 这 件 外套。

I don't like to wear this jacket.

qǐng tuō(diào) nǐ de xiézi.

请 脱(掉) 你 的 鞋子。

Please take off your shoes.

23.

Wear: dài 戴

Common expressions with "dài" (wear):

wear a hat: dài màozi 戴帽子

wear a scarf: dài wéijīn 戴围巾

wear gloves: dài shǒutào 戴手套

wear a watch: dài shǒubiǎo 戴手表

wear a necklace: dài xiàngliàn 戴项链

wear a ring: dài jièzhǐ 戴戒指

wear glasses: dài yǎnjìng 戴眼镜

wear earphones: dài ěrjī 戴耳机

24.

Give/To/For: gěi 给

Give (gifts): sònggěi 送给

For (somebody): wèi 为

To/Towards (somebody): duì 对

wǒ mèimei gěi le wǒ yí ge píngguǒ.

我 妹妹 给 了 我 一 个 苹果。

My sister gave me an apple. / My sister gave an apple to me.

tā jiè le tā de zìxíngchē gěi wǒ.

她借了她的自行车给我。

She lent her bike to me.

zhèxiē wénjiàn shì gěi nǐ de.

这些文件是给你的。

These documents are for you.

wǒ bàba gěi wǒ mǎi le yì běn shū.

我爸爸给我买了一本书。

My father bought a book for me.

(lit. My father for me bought a book.)

wǒ sònggěi tā yí ge shēngrì lǐwù.

我送给他一个生日礼物。

I gave him a birthday gift.

zhè shì wǒ wèi nǐ zuò de shēngrì dàngāo.

这是我为你做的生日蛋糕。

This is the birthday cake I made for you.

(lit. This is I for you made's birthday cake.)

tāmen shuō tāmen yīnggāi wèi rénmín fúwù.

他们说他们应该为人民服务。

They said they should serve for the people.

(lit. They said they should for the people serve.)

tā duì tāmen hěn hǎo.

她对他们很好。

She is very nice to them.

(lit. She to them very good/nice.)

25.

Hold/Take/Bring: ná 拿

Bring: dài 带

Take: dài(shàng) 带(上)

nǐ kěyǐ bāng wǒ ná yí xià zhè běn shū ma?

你可以帮我拿一下这本书吗?

Can you help me to hold this book for a moment?

(lit. You can help me hold a moment this book?)

wǒ huì ná yì zhāng DVD gěi nǐ.

我会拿一张DVD给你。

I will bring a DVD for you.

qǐng názǒu zhèxiē dōngxī.

请 拿走 这些 东西。

Please take away these things.

(lit. Please take go these things.)

wǒ huì dài jǐ ge péngyǒu lái cānjiā nǐ de shēngrì pàiduì.

我 会 带 几 个 朋友 来 参加 你 的 生日 派对。

I will bring several friends to join your birthday party.

(lit. I will bring several friends come join your birthday party.)

shīfu, qǐng dài wǒ qù fēijī chǎng.

师傅，请 带 我 去 飞机 场。

Driver, please take me to the airport.

jīntiān huì xiàyǔ. nǐ yīnggāi dài(shàng) yǔsǎn.

今天 会 下雨。你 应该 带(上) 雨伞。

It's going to rain today. You should take an umbrella.

(lit. Today will rain. You should bring umbrella.)

26.

Borrow…from (some place): cóng…jiè… 从…借…

Borrow…from (somebody): gēn/xiàng…jiè… 跟/向…借…

Lend…to…: jiè…gěi… 借…给…

Return to / Give back to: huán 还 / huángěi 还给

wǒ cóng túshūguǎn jiè le yì běn shū.

我 从 图书馆 借 了 一 本 书。

I borrowed a book from the library.

(lit. I from library borrowed one book.)

tā gēn/xiàng wǒ jiè le yì bǎ yǔsǎn.

她跟/向我借了一把雨伞。

She borrowed an umbrella from me.

(lit. She from me borrowed one umbrella.)

míngtiān shàngwǔ nǐ kěyǐ jiè nǐ de chē gěi wǒ ma?

明天上午你可以借你的车给我吗?

Could you lend your car to me tomorrow morning?

(lit. Tomorrow morning you can lend your car to me?)

míngtiān xiàwǔ wǒ huì huángěi nǐ.

明天下午我会还给你。

I will return it / give it back to you tomorrow afternoon.

(lit. Tomorrow afternoon I will return / give back to you.)

27.

Plan: jìhuà 计划 / dǎsuàn 打算

Intend: dǎsuàn 打算

Arrange: ānpái 安排

tāmen jìhuà míngnián qù àodàlìyà lǚxíng.

他们 计划 明年 去 澳大利亚 旅行。

They plan to travel to Australia next year.

(lit. They plan next year go/to Australia travel.)

wǒmen dǎsuàn liǎng ge xīngqī hòu líkāi.

我们 打算 两 个 星期 后 离开。

We intend to leave in two weeks.

(lit. We intend two weeks later leave.)

tāmen ānpái dì èr tiān jiànmiàn.

他们 安排 第 二 天 见面。

They arranged to meet the next day.

(lit. They arranged the second day meet.)

tā zhèngzài ānpái míngtiān huìyì de xìjié.

她 正在 安排 明天 会议 的 细节。

She is arranging the details for tomorrow's meeting.

(lit. She is arranging tomorrow meeting's details.)

28.

Cancel: qǔxiāo 取消

Postpone: tuīchí 推迟

Delete: shānchú 删除

wǎnshàng shí diǎn de hángbān bèi qǔxiāo le.

晚上十点的航班被取消了。(bèi + verb: passive tense)

The 10p.m. flight was cancelled.

(lit. Evening 10 o'clock's flight was cancelled.)

jīnglǐ qǔxiāo le yuējiàn kèhù.

经理取消了约见客户。

The manager cancelled the appointment with the customer.

(lit. Manager cancelled appointment customer.)

xiàwǔ liǎng diǎn de huìyì bèi tuīchí dào xiàwǔ sān diǎn bàn.

下午两点的会议被推迟到下午三点半。(bèi + verb: passive tense)

The 2p.m. meeting has been postponed to 3:30p.m..

(lit. Afternoon 2 o'clock's meeting been postponed to afternoon 3 o'clock half.)

wǒ bù xiǎoxīn shānchú le shǒujī lǐ suǒyǒu de zhàopiàn.

我 不 小心 删除 了 手机 里 所有 的 照片。

I carelessly deleted all the photos in the phone.

(lit. I not careful deleted hand machine in/inside all photos.)

29.

Reply (message, email, phone call, etc): huífù 回复

Answer (question): huídá 回答

Answer a call: jiē diànhuà 接电话

shàng ge xīngqī wǒ huífù le nǐ de diànzǐ yóujiàn.

上 个 星期 我 回复 了 你 的 电子 邮件。

I replied to your email last week.

(lit. Last week I replied your electronic mail.)

lǎoshī huídá le tā xuéshēng wèn de suǒyǒu de wèntí.

老师 回答 了 他 学生 问 的 所有 的 问题。

The teacher answered all the questions his students asked him.

(lit. Teacher answered he students asked all questions.)

kāihuì de shíhòu wǒmen bù kěyǐ jiē diànhuà.

开会 的 时候 我们 不 可以 接 电话。

We cannot answer phone calls (when) in the meeting.

(lit. Have a meeting when we cannot pick up/answer phone.)

30.

Pick up: jiē 接

See off: sòng 送 (some non English-speaking foreigners don't know what this phrase means. See off: to accompany someone to the point of departure for a trip and say good-bye upon departure)

wǒ qù huǒchē zhàn jiē wǒ de péngyǒu le.

我 去 火 车 站 接 我 的 朋 友 了。

I went to the train station to pick my friends up.

(lit. I went train station pick up my friends.)

wǒ de fùmǔ qù jīchǎng sòng wǒ le.

我 的 父 母 去 机 场 送 我 了。

My parents went to the airport to see me off.

(lit. My parents went airport see off me.)

31.

Send (message, email, etc): fā 发

Send/Post (package): jì 寄

Send/Deliver: sòng 送

Send (people to do something): pài 派

wǒ de zhùlǐ míngtiān huì fā diànzǐ yóujiàn gěi nǐ.

我的助理明天会发电子邮件给你。

My assistant will send you an email tomorrow.

(lit. My assistant tomorrow will send electronic mail to/give you.)

wǒ jì le yìxiē shèngdàn lǐwù gěi tāmen.

我寄了一些圣诞礼物给他们。

I posted some Christmas gifts to them.

sòng huò shàng mén.

送货上门。

Home delivery.

(lit. Deliver goods up door.)

zhè ge jiājù shāngdiàn kěyǐ bāng nǐ sòng huò shàng mén.

这个家具商店可以帮你送货上门。

This furniture store can help deliver the goods to your home.

(lit. This furniture store can help you deliver goods up door.)

wǒmen de lǎobǎn pài le yí ge sījī/shīfu qù fēijī chǎng jiē yí ge zhòngyào de kèhù.

我们的老板派了一个司机/师傅去飞机场接一个重要的客户。

Our boss sent a driver to pick up an important customer at the airport.

(lit. Our boss sent a driver to/go airport pick up an important customer.)

32.

Finished: verb + wán 完

Finish: wánchéng 完成 / jiéshù 结束

wǒ kàn wán zhè běn shū le.

我看完这本书了。

I have finished reading this book.

(lit. I looked finished this book.)

háizimen zuò wán yóuxì le.

孩子们做完游戏了。

The children have finished the game.

(lit. Children did finished game.)

wǒmen chī wán wǎnfàn yǐhòu qù sànbù.

我们吃完晚饭以后去散步。

We go for a walk after finishing dinner.

(lit. We eat finished dinner after/later go take a walk.)

wǒ zuò wán wǒ de gōngzuò le.

我做完我的工作了。

= wǒ wánchéng le wǒ de gōngzuò.

= 我完成了我的工作。

I finished my work.

(lit. I did finished my work.)

tāmen gānggāng kāi wán huì le.

他们刚刚开完会了。

= tāmen gānggāng jiéshù le huìyì.

= 他们刚刚结束了会议。

They just finished the meeting.

(lit. They just opened finished meeting.)

33.

Broken / Not working: huài le 坏了

tā de chē huài le.

他 的 车 坏 了。

His car is broken.

diànshìjī huài le.

电视机 坏 了。

The TV is not working.

wǒ de shǒujī tūrán huài le.

我 的 手机 突然 坏 了。

My cell phone was suddenly not working.

34.

Forget: wàngjì 忘记

Forgot: wàng le 忘了

Remember: jìde 记得 / **jìzhù** 记住

Memorize: jìzhù 记住

bié wàngjì dài yàoshi.

别忘记带钥匙。

Don't forget to take the keys.

wǒ wàng le guān chuāng.

我忘了关窗。

I forgot to close the windows.

wǒ jìde nǐ de míngzì.

我 记得 你的 名字。

I remember your name.

wǒ huì jìzhù nǐ de shēngrì.

我 会 记住 你的 生日。

I will remember your birthday.

tā jìzhù le hěnduō zhōngwén dāncí.

他 记住 了 很多 中文 单词。

He has memorized lots of Chinese vocabulary.

35.

Unable to perform the action for some reason: …bùliǎo …不了

In this situation, if two Chinese characters "了" are used together in a sentence, one should be pronounced "liǎo" and the other "le".

wǒ qù bùliǎo, yīnwèi wǒ de tuǐ shòushāng le.

我去不了，因为我的腿受伤了。

I can't go because my leg was hurt.

(lit. I go can't/unable, because my leg was hurt.)

tā yídìng zǒu bùliǎo nàme yuǎn.

他一定走不了那么远。

He is certainly unable to walk that far.

(lit. He certainly walk unable that far.)

wǒ chī bùliǎo. tài duō le.

我吃不了。太多了。

I can't eat it. It's too much.

(lit. I eat can't/unable. Too much.)

tāmen shòu bùliǎo le.

他们受不了了。

They cannot stand it.

(lit. They bear cannot/unable.)

36.

Used to (do something): céngjīng 曾经

Be/Get used to (something/doing something): xíguàn 习惯

Habit: xíguàn 习惯

wǒ céngjīng zài dàxué gōngzuò.

我曾经在大学工作。

I used to work in the university (but not any more).

(lit. I used to in university work.)

tā céngjīng měi tiān pǎobù.

他 曾经 每 天 跑步。

He used to run every day (but not any more).

(lit. He used to every day running.)

tāmen xíguàn měi tiān yòng diànnǎo.

他们 习惯 每 天 用 电脑。

They are used to using the computer every day.

(lit. They are used to every day using computer.)

nǐ huì xíguàn zhù zài zhōngguó.

你 会 习惯 住 在 中国。

You will get used to living in China.

tāmen xíguàn měi tiān wǎnshàng qī diǎn chī wǎnfàn.

他们 习惯 每 天 晚上 七 点 吃 晚饭。

It's their habit to have dinner at 7 every evening.

(lit. They habit every day evening 7 o'clock eat dinner.)

hē jiǔ biànchéng le tāmen de xíguàn.

喝 酒 变 成 了 他们 的 习惯。

Drinking has become a habit with them.

(lit. Drinking became their habit.)

37.

Change/Reform/Correct (something): gǎi 改

(Somebody/Something) Change: gǎibiàn 改变 / biàn 变

Change (job, clothes, hair style): huàn 换

Exchange (money): (duì)huàn (兑)换

qǐng bāng wǒ gǎi yí xià wǒ de hángbān.

请帮我改一下我的航班。

Please help me to change my flight.

(lit. Please help me change a moment my flight.)

juédìng zhīhòu, nǐ bù yīnggāi gǎibiàn nǐ de zhǔyì.

决定之后，你不应该改变你的主意。

After making the decision, you should not change your mind.

(lit. Make decision after, you not should change your ideas.)

tā biàn le. tā bǐ yǐqián gèng kāixīn le.

她变了。她比以前更开心了。

She changed. She is happier than before.

(lit. She changed. She than before happier.)

qíngkuàng biàn le.

情况 变 了。

The circumstances/situations changed.

tā huàn le fàxíng.

他 换 了 发型。

He changed his hair style.

(lit. He changed hair style.)

nǐ huì huàn gōngzuò ma?

你 会 换 工作 吗?

Will you change your job?

(lit. You will change job?)

wǒ xūyào (duì)huàn yìxiē gǎngbì.

我 需要 (兑)换 一些 港币。

I need to exchange some Hong Kong dollars.

38.

Become: chéngwéi 成为 / biànchéng 变成

Have/Has become: biànde 变得

(1) "chéngwéi" / "biànchéng" (become) follows a noun to express a result.

tā xiǎng chéngwéi fēixíngyuán.

他 想 成为 飞行员。

He wants to become a pilot.

tāmen biànchéng le péngyǒu.

他们 变成 了 朋友。

They became friends

(2) "biànde" (have/has become) follows an adjective to describe the situation/state has changed.

tiānqì biànde gèng rè.

天气 变得 更 热。

The weather has become hotter.

yīnwèi zuò yùndòng tāmen biànde gèng jiànkāng.

因为 做 运动 他们 变得 更 健康。

They have become healthier because of doing sports.

(lit. Because do sports they have become healthier.)

Adverbs

In Chinese, adverbs are generally put before verbs or adjectives.

wǒ fēicháng xǐhuān zhè ge dìfāng.

我 非常 喜欢 这 个 地方。

I like this place very much.

(lit. I very much like this place.)

tā kěnéng bú qù.

她 可能 不 去。

Perhaps she won't go.

(lit. She perhaps won't go.)

tiānqì hěn cháoshī.

天气 很 潮湿。

It's very humid.

(lit. Weather very humid.)

zhè ge fángzi fēicháng piàoliàng.

这 个 房子 非常 漂亮。

This house is extremely beautiful.

1.

"de" 得

(1) "de" follows a verb and precedes an adverb to describe how an action is generally performed or how it was performed in the past. The negative form is made by adding "bù" before the adverb.

shìqíng jìnzhǎn de hěn hǎo.

事情 进展 得 很 好。

Things are going/proceeding very well.

tā kāichē kāi de hěn màn.

她开车开得很慢。

She drives slowly.

(lit. She drives a car drive very slowly.)

tā pǎo de hěn kuài.

他跑得很快。

He ran very fast.

tā chī de bú kuài.

她吃得不快。

She doesn't eat fast.

(lit. She eats not fast.)

(2) "de" can be put between two verbs to express the capability. The negative form is made by changing "de" into "bù".

wǒ tīng de dǒng.

我听得懂。

I understand.

(*lit. I listen and understand.*)

wǒ tīng bù dǒng.

我听不懂。

I don't understand.

(*lit. I listen not understand.*)

wǒ kàn de dǒng.

我看得懂。

I can understand it.

(*lit. I read/look and understand.*)

wǒ kàn bù dǒng.

我看不懂。

I don't understand it.

(*lit. I read/look not understand.*)

2.

Adverbs with "de": fùcí hé "de" 副词和"地"

tā rènzhēn de xuéxí zhōngwén.

他认真地学习中文。

He studies Chinese diligently/conscientiously.

(*lit. He diligently/conscientiously studies Chinese.*)

tā zài mànmàn de xiě hànzì.

她在慢慢地写汉字。

She is slowly writing Chinese characters.

háizimen gāoxìng de zài gōngyuán lǐ wán.

孩子们高兴地在公园里玩。

The children are playing happily in the park.

(lit. Children happily in park play.)

tāmen kuàilè de shēnghuó.

他们快乐地生活。

They live happily.

(lit. They happily live.)

3.

Degree adverbs: chéngdù fùcí 程度副词

The list below outlines the degree of adverbs from "tǐng" (quite/pretty/fairly) rising to "tài" (too):

quite/pretty/fairly: tǐng 挺

very: hěn 很 / hǎo 好

really: zhēnde 真的

so (this), that: zhème 这么, nàme 那么

especially: tèbié 特别

extremely = very very / very much: fēicháng 非常 / xiāngdāng 相当

too: tài 太

zhèxiē tiān wǒ tǐng máng.

这些天我挺忙。

I am quite/pretty/fairly busy these days.

(lit. These days I quite/pretty/fairly busy.)

zhèxiē tiān wǒ hěn/hǎo máng.

这些天我很/好忙。

I am very busy these days.

(lit. These days I very busy.)

zhèxiē tiān wǒ zhēnde hěn máng.

这些天我真的很忙。

I am really busy these days.

(lit. These days I really very busy.)

zhèxiē tiān wǒ zhème máng.

这些天我这么忙。

I am so busy these days.

(lit. These days I so busy.)

zhèxiē tiān wǒ tèbié máng.

这些天我特别忙。

I am especially busy these days.

(lit. These days I especially busy.)

zhèxiē tiān wǒ fēicháng/xiāngdāng máng.

这些天我非常/相当忙。

I am extremely busy these days.

(lit. These days I extremely busy.)

zhèxiē tiān wǒ tài máng le.

这些天我太忙了。

I am too busy these days.

(lit. These days I too busy.)

4.

Extremely: fēicháng 非常 (formal) / sǐ le 死了 (informal, negative adverbs only)

extremely busy: fēicháng máng 非常忙

máng sǐ le 忙死了 *(lit. busy death)*

extremely hungry: fēicháng è 非常饿

è sǐ le 饿死了 *(lit. hungry death)*

extremely tired: fēicháng lèi 非常累

lèi sǐ le 累死了 *(lit. tired death)*

extremely annoyed: fēicháng fán 非常烦

   fán sǐ le 烦死了 *(lit. annoyed death)*

extremely cold: fēicháng lěng 非常冷

   lěng sǐ le 冷死了 *(lit. cold death)*

5.

How can somebody/something be so/that + adjective: …zěnme zhème/nàme… …怎么这么/那么…

tā zěnme zhème hǎo!

她 怎 么 这 么 好!

How can she be so nice!

(lit. She how so nice!)

tā zěnme nàme bù xiǎoxīn!

他怎么那么不小心!

How can he be that careless!

(lit. He how that not careful!)

nǐ zěnme zhème máng!

你怎么这么忙!

How can you be so busy!

(lit. You how so busy!)

fángjiān zěnme nàme zāng!

房间怎么那么脏!

How can the room be that dirty!

(lit. Room how that dirty!)

6.

Really: zhēnde 真的 / zhēn 真

tāmen zhēnde xiǎng xuéxí zhōngwén.

他们 真的 想 学习 中文。

They really want to learn Chinese.

jīntiān tiānqì zhēn rè.

今天 天气 真 热。

It's really hot today.

(lit. Today weather really hot.)

7.

Too/Also/Either: yě 也

tā yě hěn gāo.

他也很高。

He is also very tall.

wǒ yě qù guò nàlǐ.

我也去过那里。

I have been there, too. / I have also been there.

(lit. I too/also have been there.)

tāmen yě bú huì qù.

他们也不会去。

They won't go either.

(lit. They either not will go.)

8.

Both/All: dōu 都

None / All not: dōu méi 都没 / **dōu bù** 都不

Not all: bù dōu 不都

("All" can also be an adjective. Refer to BOOK 1 "Common Adjectives and Their Relative Words" 9)

wǒmen dōu xué zhōngwén.

我们 都 学 中文。

We all study Chinese.

tā hé wǒ dōu xǐhuān yǔyán.

他 和 我 都 喜欢 语言。

He and I both like languages.

wǒ bàba māma dōu tuìxiū le.

我 爸爸 妈妈 都 退休 了。

My father and my mother are both retired.

(lit. My father mother both retired.)

tāmen (liǎng ge rén) dōu méiyǒu qù.

他们(两 个 人) 都 没有 去。

They both didn't go.

tāmen dōu méi shàng guò dàxué.

他们 都 没 上 过 大学。

They all have not attended university.

= None of them have attended university.

háizimen dōu bú yuànyì shuìjiào.

孩子们 都 不 愿意 睡觉。

The children are all not willing to sleep.

= None of the children are willing to sleep.

wǒmen dōu bú huì kāichē.

我们 都 不 会 开车。

We all cannot drive.

wǒmen bù dōu huì kāichē. yìxiē huì, yìxiē bú huì.

我们 不 都 会 开车。一些 会，一些 不 会。

We cannot all drive a car. Some can, some cannot.

= Not all of us can drive a car. Some can, some cannot.

(lit. We not all can drive a car. Some can, some cannot.)

wǒmen bù dōu shì měiguórén. tā shì yīngguórén. wǒ shì zhōngguórén. zhǐyǒu tā shì měiguórén.

我们 不 都 是 美国人。他 是 英国人。我 是 中国人。只有 她 是 美国人。

We are not all Americans. He is English. I am Chinese. Only she is American.

= Not all of us are Americans. He is English. I am Chinese. Only she is American.

(lit. We not all are Americans. He is English. I am Chinese. Only she is American.)

In Chinese, question word "shénme" (what) + noun + "dōu" (all) is commonly used to convey the meaning "every" or "any".

tā shénme shìqíng dōu dǒng.

他 什么 事情 都 懂。

He understands everything.

(lit. He what things all understands.)

tā shénme shìqíng dōu bù dǒng.

他什么事情都不懂。

He doesn't understand anything.

(lit. He what things all doesn't understand.)

zhōngguó rénkǒu dà. shénme dìfāng dōu shì rén.

中国人口大。什么地方都是人。

China's population is big. There are people everywhere.

(lit. China population big. What place all are people.)

shénme shíhòu dōu kěyǐ.

什么时候都可以。

Anytime is ok.

(lit. What time/When all ok.)

9.

Still : hái 还 / réngrán 仍然

Else: hái 还

tāmen hái zhù zài zhèlǐ.

他们还住在这里。

They are still living here.

(lit. They still live here.)

bànyè le. tā hái zài gōngzuò.

半夜了。他还在工作。

It's midnight. He is still working.

(lit. Half night. He still is working.)

tāmen réngrán zhù zài tóngyàng de chéngshì.

他们仍然住在同样的城市。

They still live in the same city.

nǐ hái xiǎng mǎi shénme?

你还想买什么?

What else do you want to buy?

(lit. You still want buy what?)

hái yào bié de dōngxī ma? / hái yǒu bié de shìqíng ma?

还要别的东西吗? / 还有别的事情吗?

Anything else?

(lit. Still want other things? / Still have other things?)

(the difference between "dōngxī" (things) and "shìqíng" (things), refer to "Common Verbs and Their Usages" 12 in this book)

10.

Haven't...yet: hái méiyǒu... 还没有...

tāmen hái méiyǒu xiàbān.

他们还没有下班。

They haven't finished work yet.

(lit. They yet/still haven't finished work.)

wǒ hái méiyǒu kàn wán zhè běn shū.

我还没有看完这本书。

I haven't finished reading this book yet.

(lit. I yet/still haven't read finished this book.)

11.

Have already: yǐjīng 已经

tāmen yǐjīng chūfā le.

他们已经出发了。

They have already started off.

wǒ yǐjīng kàn guò nà běn shū.

我已经看过那本书。

I have already read that book.

12.

Only: zhǐ(yǒu) 只(有)

tā zhǐ(yǒu) zài zhè ge gōngsī gōngzuò guò.

她只(有)在这个公司工作过。

She has worked only in this company.

(lit. She only in this company has worked.)

tā zhǐyǒu èrshí suì, dànshì tā qù guò hěnduō qítā guójiā.

他只有二十岁，但是他去过很多其它国家。

He is only 20, but he has been to lots of other countries.

(lit. He only 20 years old, but he has been to lots of other countries.)

tā zhǐyǒu yì zhī bǐ.

他只有一支笔。

He only has a pen.

tāmen zhǐ xǐhuān zhè ge cāntīng.

他们只喜欢这个餐厅。

They only like this restaurant.

wǒ zhǐyào yì bēi bīng shuǐ

我只要一杯冰水。

I only want a glass of ice water.

13.

Just: gāng(gāng) 刚(刚) (Something happened a moment ago.)

Just right: gānggāng hǎo 刚刚好

Only just: cái 才 (Something should have happened earlier, but it's too late to do anything about it.)

tā gānggāng dào le gōngsī.

他 刚刚 到 了 公司。

He just arrived at the company.

wǒmen gāng kāi wán huì le.

我们 刚 开 完 会 了。

We just finished the meeting.

(lit. We just opened finished meeting.)

wǎng zuǒ yí yìdiǎn. xiànzài gānggāng hǎo.

往左移一点。现在刚刚好。

Move a little to the left. Now it's just right.

(lit. Toward/To left move a little. Now just good.)

tā shíyī diǎn cái dào gōngsī.

他十一点才到公司。

He only just arrived at the company at 11 o'clock.

(lit. He 11 o'clock only just arrived company.)

fēijī yí ge xiǎoshí hòu cái qǐfēi.

飞机一个小时后才起飞。

The plane only just took off after an hour.

(lit. Plane one hour later only just took off.)

14.

A little / A little bit + adjective: yǒudiǎn 有点

Verb + A little / A little bit: yìdiǎn 一点 **/ yìdiǎndiǎn** 一点点

Verb + (a little / a little bit) + comparative degree of adverbs:

 …yìdiàn …一点

zhè dào cài yǒudiǎn là.

这 道 菜 有点 辣。

This dish is a little bit spicy.

kāfēi yǒudiǎn rè.

咖啡 有点 热。

The coffee is a little hot.

tāmen huì shuō yìdiǎndiǎn zhōngwén.

他们 会 说 一点点 中文。

They can speak a little bit Chinese.

wǒ hē le yìdiǎn shuǐ.

我 喝 了 一点 水。

I drank a little water.

qǐng zǒu kuài yìdiǎn.

请 走 快 一点。

Please walk (a little) faster.

(lit. Please walk fast a little.)

nǐ yīnggāi chī màn yìdiǎn.

你 应该 吃 慢 一点。

You should eat (a little bit) more slowly.

(lit. You should eat slowly a little bit.)

15.

A moment: yí xià 一下 / yí huì 一会 (It implies that the action lasts for a short time.)

wǒ xiǎng zuò yí xià / yí huì.

我 想 坐 一下 / 一会。

I want to sit for a moment.

shīfu, qǐng tíng yí xià / yí huì.

师傅，请 停 一下 / 一会。

Driver, please stop for a moment.

qǐng děng wǒ yí xià / yí huì.

请等我一下 / 一会。

Please wait me for a moment.

16.

Together: yìqǐ 一起

tāmen xǐhuān yìqǐ guàngjiē.

她们喜欢一起逛街。

They like to go shopping together.

(lit. They like together go shopping / look around streets.)

wǒmen yìqǐ qù chīfàn.

我们一起去吃饭。

Let's go to eat together.

(lit. We together go eat.)

17.

First…and then…: xiān 先…, ránhòu 然后…

wǒmen xiān qù chīfàn, ránhòu qù kàn diànyǐng.

我们 先 去 吃饭，然后 去 看 电影。

We go to eat first, and then go to watch a movie.

(lit. We first go eat, then go watch movie.)

wǒmen yīnggāi xiān kǎolǜ, ránhòu zài juédìng.

我们 应该 先 考虑，然后 再 决定。

We should think about it first, and then make a decision.

(lit. We should first think about, then again decide.)

18.

Ago: qián 前

Later: hòu 后

Before: yǐqián 以前 / zhīqián 之前

After: yǐhòu 以后 / zhīhòu 之后

sì nián qián wǒ qù le àodàlìyà.

四年前我去了澳大利亚。

I went to Australia 4 years ago.

(lit. 4 years ago I went Australia.)

yí ge xīngqī hòu tāmen huílái le.

一个星期后他们回来了。

They came back a week later.

(lit. One week later they back came.)

shàngbān yǐqián/zhīqián tā zǒngshì xǐhuān hē yì bēi kāfēi.

上班 以前/之前 他 总是 喜欢 喝 一 杯 咖啡。

He always likes to drink a cup of coffee before going to work.

(lit. Go to work before he always likes drink a cup coffee.)

wǒmen chīfàn yǐhòu/zhīhòu qù kàn diànyǐng.

我们 吃饭 以后/之后 去 看 电影。

After we eat, we will go to watch a movie.

(lit. We eat after go watch movie.)

19.

Sometimes: yǒu shíhòu 有时候

Usually: tōngcháng 通常 / **píngshí** 平时

Often: jīngcháng 经常

Very often: chángcháng 常常

Always / All the time: zǒngshì 总是

yǒu shíhòu tā qù dǎ lánqiú.

有时候 他 去 打 篮球。

Sometimes he goes to play basketball.

xiàbān zhīhòu nǐ tōngcháng zuò shénme?

下班 之后 你 通常 做 什么?

What do you usually do after work?

(lit. Finish work after you usually do what?)

tā jīngcháng qù běijīng chūchāi.

他 经常 去 北京 出差。

He often goes to Beijing for business trips.

tāmen chángcháng qù pǎobù.

他们 常常 去 跑步。

They go running very often.

(lit. They very often go running.)

zǒngshì bàoyuàn bù hǎo.

总是 抱怨 不 好。

It's not good to complain all the time.

(lit. Always/All the time complaining not good.)

20.

Recently: zuìjìn 最近 / jìnlái 近来

Actually / In fact: shìshí shàng 事实上

Generally speaking: yìbān lái shuō 一般来说

Unfortunately: hěn búxìng 很不幸

nǐ zuìjìn zěnmeyàng?

你最近怎么样?

How have you been recently?

(lit. You recently how?)

shìshí shàng wǒ bú rènshí tāmen.

事实上我不认识他们。

Actually/In fact I don't know them.

yìbān lái shuō, qī yuè tiānqì hěn rè.

一般来说,七月天气很热。

Generally speaking, it's very hot in July.

(lit. So-so come say, July weather very hot.)

hěn búxìng, tā fāshāo le.

很不幸，她发烧了。

Unfortunately she has a fever.

(lit. Very not lucky, she has a fever.)

21.

Again: yòu 又 (used for past tense)

Again: zài 再 (used for present tense and future tense)

Didn't/Never…again: méiyǒu zài… 没有再… (used for past tense)

Not…any more / No more: bú zài… 不再… (used for present tense and future tense)

"yòu" (again) is used for an actual action which happened again (past tense).

"zài" (again) is used for an action that will happen again (present tense and future tense).

tā yòu gǎnmào le.

她又感冒了。

She had a cold again.

(lit. She again had a cold.)

tā zuótiān lái le. jīntiān xiàwǔ yòu lái le.

他昨天来了。今天下午又来了。

He came yesterday. This afternoon he came again.

(lit. He yesterday came. Today afternoon again came.)

qǐng zài shuō yí biàn.

请再说一遍。

Please say it again.

(lit. Please again say one time.)

xià ge yuè wǒ zài lái kàn nǐ.

下个月我再来看你。

I will come to visit you again next month.

(lit. Next month I again come see/visit you.)

tā méiyǒu zài qù nà ge gōngsī shàngbān le.

他没有再去那个公司上班了。

He didn't go to work in that company again.

(lit. He didn't again go that company work.)

tā bú zài chōuyān.

他不再抽烟。

He doesn't smoke any more.

(lit. He doesn't again smoke.)

tā bú zài xiāngxìn tāmen.

他不再相信他们。

He won't believe them any more.

(lit. He won't again believe them.)

22.

Again and again: yí biàn yòu yí biàn de 一遍又一遍地 (concerning the same things/contents each time)

Again and again: yí cì yòu yí cì de 一次又一次地 (concerning different methods to accomplish the same result)

xuéshēngmen yí biàn yòu yí biàn de kàn zhè běn shū.

学生们一遍又一遍地看这本书。

The students read this book again and again.

(lit. Students again and again read this book.)

tā yí biàn yòu yí biàn de kàn zhè bù diànyǐng.

他一遍又一遍地看这部电影。

He watches this movie again and again.

(lit. He again and again watches this movie.)

tāmen yí cì yòu yí cì de xiè tā.

他们一次又一次地谢他。

They thank him again and again.

(lit. They again and again thank him.)

23.

Less than/Under: bú dào 不到

More than/Over: duō 多

tāmen zhù zài zhèlǐ bú dào yí ge yuè.

他们住在这里不到一个月。

They have lived here less than one month.

zài yìxiē xīfāng guójiā, bú dào shíbā suì de qīngshàonián bù kěyǐ mǎi jiǔ.

在一些西方国家,不到十八岁的青少年不可以买酒。

In some western countries, teenagers cannot buy alcohol if they are under 18.

(lit. In some western countries, under 18 years old teenagers cannot buy alcohol.)

tāmen de gōngsī yǒu yìbǎi duō ge yuángōng.

他们的公司有一百多个员工。

Their company has more than 100 staff.

(lit. Their company has 100 many staff.)

wǒ de nǎinai bāshí duō suì.

我 的 奶奶 八十 多 岁。

My grandmother is over 80 years old.

(lit. My grandmother 80 many years old.)

24.

At least: zhìshǎo 至少

At most: zhìduō 至多

tāmen zhìshǎo huì zài zhōngguó zhù sān nián.

他们 至少 会 在 中国 住 三 年。

They will live in China for at least 3 years.

(lit. They at least will in China live 3 years.)

wǒ cāi xiànzài zhìduō shíyī diǎn.

我 猜 现在 至多 十一 点。

I guess it's at most 11 o'clock now.

(lit. I guess now at most 11 o'clock.)

tā zhìshǎo èrshíwǔ suì.

她 至少 二十五 岁。

She is at least 25 years old.

tā zhìduō èrshíwǔ suì.

她 至多 二十五 岁。

She is at most 25 years old.

25.

Almost: chàbùduō 差不多 / jīhū 几乎

About/Around/More or less: dàgài + number 大概 / number + zuǒyòu 左右

About/On/Concerning/Regarding: guānyú 关于 (preposition)

tāmen děng le chàbùduō/jīhū yí ge xiǎoshí.

他们 等 了 差不多/几乎 一 个 小时。

They waited for almost one hour.

wǒ chàbùduō chídào le.

我 差不多 迟到 了。

I am almost late.

zhè ge gōngsī yǒu dàgài yìbǎi èrshí ge yuángōng.

这 个 公司 有 大概 一百 二十 个 员工。

There is about 120 staff in this company.

(lit. This company has about 120 staff.)

wǒ de qiánbāo yǒu sānbǎi yuán zuǒyòu.

我的钱包有三百元左右。

There's around / more or less 300 *yuan* in my wallet.

(lit. My money bag has 300 yuan left right.)

zhè shì yì běn guānyú zhōngguó de shū.

这是一本关于中国的书。

This is a book about China.

(lit. This is one about China's book.)

26.

Not...at all: gēnběn bù... 根本不… / wánquán bù... 完全不…

Completely: wánquán 完全

wǒ gēnběn bú rènshí tāmen.

我 根本 不 认识 他们。

I don't know them at all.

(lit. I at all don't know them.)

wǒ gēnběn bù zhīdào.

我 根本 不 知道。

= wǒ wánquán bù zhīdào.

= 我 完全 不 知道。

I have no idea at all.

(lit. I at all don't know. = I completely don't know.)

zìmù tài xiǎo. wǒ gēnběn kàn bú jiàn.

字幕 太 小。我 根本 看 不 见。

The subtitles are too small. I can't see them at all.

(lit. Subtitles too small. I at all see not.)

tā de tuǐ wánquán huīfù le.

他的腿完全恢复了。

His leg completely recovered.

Interjections

Mandarin uses interjections at the beginning of the sentence and at the end of the sentence to indicate the feeling of the speaker towards the situation expressed. Feelings include surprise, suggestion, agreement, regret, etc. The omission or inclusion of the interjections doesn't affect the grammatical status of the sentence.

1.

Here are some common interjections put at the beginning of the sentences and their associated meanings.

ā 啊 *surprise*

ā, shì nǐ ya!

啊，是你呀!

Oh, it's you!

(lit. Oh, is you!)

ā 啊 *agreement, approval, acknowledgement*

ā, nǐ shuō de duì.

啊，你说得对。

Yes. What you said is right.

(lit. Yes, you said right.)

āi 哎 *surprise, dissatisfaction*

āi, huǒchē wèishéme hái méi dào a?

哎，火车为什么还没到啊？

Oh! Why hasn't the train arrived yet?

(lit. Oh, train why yet/stil hasn't arrived.)

āiyō 哎哟 *surprise, pain*

āiyō! hǎo tòng!

哎哟！好痛！

Ouch! It hurts!

(lit. Ouch! Very painful!)

āiyā 哎呀 *wonder, shock*

āiyā! zhème wǎn le. wǒ děi zǒu le.

哎呀！这么晚了。我得走了。

Gosh! It's so late. I have to go.

(lit. Gosh! So late. I have to go.)

āyā 啊呀 *pained surprise*

āyā, wǒ de shǒujī bèi tōu le.

啊呀，我的手机被偷了。

Oh no! My mobile phone was stolen.

(lit. Oh no! My hand machine was stolen.)

āi 唉 *regret*

āi, wǒ zhēn bù yīnggāi lái.

唉，我真不应该来。

Ai, I really should not have come.

(lit. Ai, I really not should come.)

2.

Here are some common interjections put at the end of the sentences and their associated meanings. They occur in neutral tone.

ba 吧 *suggestion (when making a statement); guessing, fairly certain (when asking a question)*

wǒmen yìqǐ chī wǔfàn ba.

我们 一起 吃 午饭 吧。

Let's have lunch together.

(lit. We together eat lunch.)

nǐ shì wáng lǎoshī ba?

你 是 王 老师 吧?

Are you teacher Wang?

(lit. You are Wang teacher?)

le/lo 了/咯 *obviousness*

wǒ děi zǒu le. rúguǒ xiànzài wǒ bù zǒu, wǒ jiù huì chídào lo.

我得走了。如果现在我不走，我就会迟到咯。

I have to go. If I don't go now I will be late

(lit. I have to go. If now I don't go, I will late.)

a 啊 *obviousness, impatience*

nǐ yīnggāi duō zhùyì shēntǐ a.

你应该多注意身体啊。

You should pay more attention to your health.

(lit. You should many pay attention body.)

la 啦 *exclamation*

hǎo la! bú yào zài shuō la!

好啦！不要再说啦！

Okay! Don't say it again!

(lit. Okay! Don't again say!)

Part 2   Appendix

Common Measure Words

个 ge

(It's the most common measure word for persons, areas, units, material things, time, abstract nouns, etc. If you don't know which measure word to use, you can always use measure word "ge". It may not be strictly correct, and you may find people gently correct you, but you'll be understood.)

A person: yí ge rén 一个人

A waiter/waitress: yí ge fúwùyuán 一个服务员

A friend: yí ge péngyǒu 一个朋友

A city: yí ge chéngshì 一个城市

A school: yí ge xuéxiào 一个学校

An apple: yí ge píngguǒ 一个苹果

A vase: yí ge huāpíng 一个花瓶

A summer: yí ge xiàtiān 一个夏天

An afternoon: yí ge xiàwǔ 一个下午

A dream: yí ge mèng 一个梦

A question/problem: yí ge wèntí 一个问题

A good idea: yí ge hǎo zhǔyì 一个好主意

杯 bēi (glass/cup, to measure the quantity of liquid)

A glass of ice water: yì bēi bīng shuǐ 一杯冰水

A glass of milk: yì bēi niúnǎi 一杯牛奶

A cup of coffee: yì bēi kāfēi 一杯咖啡

A cup of tea: yì bēi chá 一杯茶

瓶 píng (bottle, to measure the quantity of liquid)

A bottle of beer: yì píng píjiǔ 一瓶啤酒

A bottle of cola: yì píng kělè 一瓶可乐

A bottle of soft drink: yì píng yǐnliào 一瓶饮料

件 jiàn (measure word for clothes, affairs/matters/invisible abstract things)

A piece of clothes: yí jiàn yīfú 一件衣服

A coat: yí jiàn dàyī 一件大衣

A jacket: yí jiàn jiákè 一件夹克

A matter/thing: yí jiàn shìqíng 一件事情

间 jiān (measure word for rooms and warehouse)

A room: yì jiān fángjiān 一间房间

A bedroom: yì jiān wòshì 一间卧室

A study: yì jiān shūfáng 一间书房

A classroom: yì jiān jiàoshì 一间教室

A washroom: yì jiān xǐshǒujiān 一间洗手间

A warehouse: yì jiān cāngkù 一间仓库

本 běn (measure word for books, magazine and notebook)

A book: yì běn shū 一本书

A dictionary: yì běn cídiǎn 一本词典

A novel: yì běn xiǎoshuō 一本小说

A magazine: yì běn zázhì 一本杂志

A notebook: yì běn bǐjìběn 一本笔记本

张 zhāng (measure word for flat things or things with a surface)

A map: yì zhāng dìtú 一张地图

A newspaper: yì zhāng bàozhǐ 一张报纸

A plane ticket: yì zhāng fēijī piào 一张飞机票

A photo/picture: yì zhāng zhàopiàn 一张照片

A card: yì zhāng kǎ 一张卡

A table/desk: yì zhāng zhuōzi 一张桌子

A sofa: yì zhāng shāfā 一张沙发

A bed: yì zhāng chuáng 一张床

辆 liàng (measure word for vehicles)

A bus: yí liàng bāshì 一辆巴士

A taxi: yí liàng díshì 一辆的士

A tram: yí liàng diànchē 一辆电车

A bicycle: yí liàng zìxíngchē 一辆自行车

A car: yí liàng qìchē 一辆汽车

部 bù (measure word for films or artistic work and telephones)

A film/movie: yí bù diànyǐng 一部电影

A TV show: yí bù diànshìjù 一部电视剧

A telephone: yí bù diànhuà 一部电话

A mobile/cell phone: yí bù shǒujī 一部手机

台 tái (measure word for machines and facilities)

A machine: yì tái jīqì 一台机器

A TV: yì tái diànshì 一台电视

A computer: yì tái diànnǎo 一台电脑

A fridge: yì tái bīngxiāng 一台冰箱

An air-conditioner: yì tái kōngtiáo 一台空调

家 jiā (measure word for family, an institution, enterprise, unit, etc)

A family (people): yì jiā rén 一家人

A bank: yì jiā yínháng 一家银行

A company: yì jiā gōngsī 一家公司

A factory: yì jiā gōngchǎng 一家工厂

A hospital: yì jiā yīyuàn 一家医院

A theater: yì jiā jùyuàn 一家剧院

A shop/store: yì jiā shāngdiàn 一家商店

把 bǎ (measure word for a thing with a handle or something like a handle)

A chair: yì bǎ yǐzi 一把椅子

An umbrella: yì bǎ yǔsǎn 一把雨伞

A comb: yì bǎ shūzi 一把梳子

A key: yì bǎ yàoshi 一把钥匙

A lock: yì bǎ suǒ 一把锁

A spoon: yì bǎ sháozi 一把勺子

A fork: yì bǎ chāzi 一把叉子

A knife: yì bǎ dāo 一把刀

包 bāo (measure word for the things wrapped or tied up and things fixed in bundles)

A package of biscuits: yì bāo bǐnggān 一包饼干

A package of tea leaves: yì bāo cháyè 一包茶叶

A bundle of matches: yì bāo huǒchái 一包火柴

A bundle of cigarettes: yì bāo yān 一包烟

袋 dài (measure word for things in a bag or sack)

A bag of milk powder: yí dài nǎifěn 一袋奶粉

A bag of flour: yí dài miànfěn 一袋面粉

A bag of rice: yí dài mǐ 一袋米

A bag of candies: yí dài tángguǒ 一袋糖果

A bag of detergent: yí dài xǐyīfěn 一袋洗衣粉

只 zhī (measure word for one of the two things of the same kind, for one of the symmetrical limbs or organs of people or animals, for insects or animals)

A glove: yì zhī shǒutào 一只手套

A shoe: yì zhī xiézi 一只鞋子

A sock: yì zhī wàzi 一只袜子

An eye: yì zhī yǎnjīng 一只眼睛

An ear: yì zhī ěrduo 一只耳朵

A hand: yì zhī shǒu 一只手

An arm: yì zhī gēbó 一只胳膊

A foot: yì zhī jiǎo 一只脚

A leg: yì zhī tuǐ 一只腿

A dog: yì zhī gǒu 一只狗

A cat: yì zhī māo 一只猫

A panda: yì zhī xióngmāo 一只熊猫

A chicken: yì zhī jī 一只鸡

头 tóu (measure word for domestic animals)

A pig: yì tóu zhū 一头猪

An ox: yì tóu niú 一头牛

A lamb: yì tóu yáng 一头羊

An elephant: yì tóu dàxiàng 一头大象

对 duì (measure word for two persons as a couple, two things associated or used together)

A married couple: yí duì fūqī 一对夫妻

A pair of vases: yí duì huāpíng 一对花瓶

A pair of pillows: yí duì zhěntóu 一对枕头

A pair of earrings: yí duì ěrhuán 一对耳环

A pair of bracelets: yí duì shǒuzhuó 一对手镯

双 shuāng (measure word for two things of the same kind to be used together, for some organs of the human body)

A pair of chopsticks: yì shuāng kuàizi 一双筷子

A pair of gloves: yì shuāng shǒutào 一双手套

A pair of leather shoes: yì shuāng píxié 一双皮鞋

A pair of socks: yì shuāng wàzi 一双袜子

A pair of feet: yì shuāng jiǎo 一双脚

A pair of hands: yì shuāng shǒu 一双手

A pair of eyes: yì shuāng yǎnjīng 一双眼睛

条 tiáo (measure word for long, narrow things)

A pair of pants: yì tiáo kùzi 一条裤子

A skirt: yì tiáo qúnzi 一条裙子

A necklace: yì tiáo xiàngliàn 一条项链

A scarf: yì tiáo wéijīn 一条围巾

A towl: yì tiáo máojīn 一条毛巾

A street: yì tiáo jiē 一条街

A rope: yì tiáo shéngzi 一条绳子

块 kuaì (measure word for pieces/slices of food-stuff, for regular-shaped products, for Chinese currency)

A piece of watermelon: yí kuài xīguā 一块西瓜

A piece of cake: yí kuài dàngāo 一块蛋糕

A piece of meat: yí kuài ròu 一块肉

A watch: yí kuài shǒubiǎo 一块手表

A piece of glass: yí kuài bōlí 一块玻璃

A coin: yí kuài yìngbì 一块硬币

One RMB: yí kuài(qián) 一块(钱) = yì yuán 一元

次 cì (measure word for the number of repetitions in a given period of time and the number of times an action is taken)

An opportunity / A chance: yí cì jīhuì 一次机会

An exam / A test: yí cì kǎoshì 一次考试

A discussion: yí cì tǎolùn 一次讨论

A date: yí cì yuēhuì 一次约会

One time: yí cì 一次

Two times: liǎng cì 两次

Several times: jǐ cì 几次

支 zhī (measure word for rod-shaped goods, songs, troops, etc)

A pen: yì zhī bǐ 一支笔

A cigarette: yì zhī yān 一支烟

A song: yì zhī gē 一支歌

A troop: yì zhī jūnduì 一支军队

封 fēng (measure word for letters, emails, etc)

A letter: yì fēng xìn 一封信

An email: yì fēng diànzi yóujiàn 一封电子邮件

套 tào (measure word for a group of things used together)

A suit: yí tào xīzhuāng 一套西装

A set of clothes: yí tào yīfú 一套衣服

A set of furniture: yí tào jiājù 一套家具

层 céng (measure word for the storeys of a building or stairs, outer covering, etc)

A floor: yì céng lóu 一层楼

A stair: yì céng jiētī 一层阶梯

A covering of ice: yì céng bīng 一层冰

A covering of snow: yì céng xuě 一层雪

A covering of cream: yì céng nǎiyóu 一层奶油

Common Words and Phrases

Are you sure: nǐ quèdìng ma 你确定吗

As soon as possible: jìnkuài 尽快

Bad luck: dǎoméi 倒霉

Bastard / Son of bitch: wángbādàn 王八蛋

Beautiful girl: měinǚ 美女

Be jealous: chīcù 吃醋

Believe it or not: xìn bú xìn yóu nǐ 信不信由你

Better than nothing: bǐ méiyǒu hǎo 比没有好

Boast: chuīniú 吹牛

Boring: wúliáo 无聊

By the way: shùnbiàn shuō yí xià 顺便说一下

Careless person: mǎdàhā 马大哈

Crazy person: shénjīngbìng 神经病

Can only imagine: zhǐ néng xiǎngxiàng 只能想象

Can't imagine: wúfǎ xiǎngxiàng 无法想象

Can't help / Can't do it: méi bànfǎ 没办法

Come on: jiāyóu 加油

Congratulations: gōngxǐ 恭喜 / zhùhè 祝贺

Disgusting: ěxīn 恶心

Don't annoy/bother me: bié fán wǒ 别烦我

Don't care: bú zàihū 不在乎 / wú suǒwèi 无所谓

Don't mind: bú jièyì 不介意

Enjoy life: xiǎngshòu shēnghuó 享受生活

Enjoy yourself / Have fun: wán de kāixīn 玩得开心

Excellent: hǎo jí le 好极了 / tài bàng le 太棒了

Flatter someone: pāi mǎpì 拍马屁

For example: bǐrú shuō 比如说

Forget it: suàn le 算了

Good idea: hǎo zhǔyì 好主意

Good news: hǎo xiāoxī 好消息

Handsome guy: shuàigē 帅哥

Hurry up: kuài diǎn 快点

It depends: kàn qíngkuàng 看情况

Idiot: báichī 白痴 / bèndàn 笨蛋 / shǎguā 傻瓜

I promise: wǒ bǎozhèng 我保证

It's a deal: yì yán wéi dìng 一言为定

It's none of your business: bù guān nǐ de shì 不关你的事

It's up to you: suíbiàn 随便

It serves someone right: huógāi 活该

Keep in touch: bǎochí liánxì 保持联系

Keep silent: bǎochí chénmò 保持沉默

Ladies first: nǚshì yōuxiān 女士优先

Leave me alone: lí wǒ yuǎn yìdiǎn 离我远一点

Let me see/think: ràng wǒ xiǎngxiǎng 让我想想

Long time no see: hǎo jiǔ bú jiàn 好久不见

Lucky: hǎoyùn 好运 / xìngyùn 幸运

Make an excuse: zhǎo jièkǒu 找借口

Make sense: yǒu dàolǐ 有道理

Make no sense: méi dàolǐ 没道理

My God: wǒ de tiān a 我的天啊

Narrow-minded: xiǎo xīnyǎn 小心眼

No comment: wú kě fènggào 无可奉告

No choice: bié wú xuǎnzé 别无选择

No reason: méi lǐyóu 没理由

No way: bù xíng 不行

No wonder: nánguài 难怪

Nonsense: hú shuō bā dào 胡说八道

Nosey: duō guǎn xiánshì 多管闲事

Nothing is impossible: méi shénme bù kěnéng 没什么不可能

On purpose: gùyì de 故意的

Out of sight, out of mind: yǎn bú jiàn, xīn bù fán 眼不看, 心不想

Perverted: biàntài 变态

Secret: mìmì 秘密

Shut up: bì zuǐ 闭嘴

Sixth sense: dì liù gǎn 第六感

Small case: xiǎo yìsī 小意思

Snobbish: shìliyǎn 势利眼

Sounds good: tīng qǐlái bú cuò 听起来不错

Step by step: yí bù yí bù lái 一步一步来

Take your time: mànmàn lái 慢慢来

Take care: bǎozhòng 保重

To be honest: shíhuà shuō 实话说

Try one's best: jìnlì 尽力

Wait and see: zǒu zhe qiáo 走着瞧

Waste time: làngfèi shíjiān 浪费时间

What a pity: zhēn kěxī 真可惜

What can we do: zěnmebàn 怎么办

What's the matter: shénme shì 什么事

Without a doubt: háo wú yíwèn 毫无疑问

You are crazy: nǐ fēng le 你疯了

You did a good job: nǐ zuò de hěn hǎo 你做得很好

You look down upon me: nǐ xiǎo kàn wǒ 你小看我

Primer on Writing Chinese Characters

1.

Names of the Strokes: bǐhuà míngchēng 笔画名称

Chinese characters consist of special strokes as shown below:

一	héng	e.g. 十
丨	shù	e.g. 中
丿	piě	e.g. 人
乀	nà	e.g. 八
丶	diǎn	e.g. 六
ノ	tí	e.g. 地
一→	héng gōu	e.g. 门

ㄱ	héng zhé	e.g. 五
ㄱ	héng zhé gōu	e.g. 月
㆗	héng zhézhézhé gōu	e.g. 仍
⁾	wān gōu	e.g. 子
乙	héng zhé wān gōu	e.g. 九
乙	héng zhé tí	e.g. 说
ㄱ	héng piě	e.g. 水
㆚	héng piě wān gōu	e.g. 队
㇄	xié gōu	e.g. 我
㇆	héng xié gōu	e.g. 气
亅	shù gōu	e.g. 小
ㄴ	shù zhé	e.g. 山

ㄅ	shù zhézhé gōu	e.g. 马
L	shù wān	e.g. 四
ㄴ	shù wān gōu	e.g. 儿
ㄴ	shù tí	e.g. 以
ㄑ	piě zhé	e.g. 去
ㄑ	piě diǎn	e.g. 女
ㄴ	wò gōu	e.g. 心

2.

The Basic Rules of the Order of Strokes: bǐhuà shùnxù de jīběn guīzé 笔画顺序的基本规则

| xiān zuǒ hòu yòu | First left, then right | e.g. 八 |

xiān zhōngjiān, hòu zuǒyòu / liǎngbiān	First center, then left and right/sides	e.g. 小
cóng shàng dào xià	First top, then bottom	e.g. 二
xiān héng hòu shù	First horizontal, then vertical	e.g. 十
xiān wài hòu lǐ	First outside, then inside	e.g. 月
xiān lǐbiān, hòu fēngkǒu	Close after filling the frame	e.g. 日

3.

33 common characters: sānshísān ge chángyòng hànzì 三十三个常用汉字

Know the order to write these 33 common characters. Then using the same methods you will know how to write others.

一 one	一				
二 two	一	二			
三 three	一	二	三		
四 four	丨	冂	冃	四	四
五 five	一	丁	五	五	
六 six	丶	亠	六	六	
七 seven	一	七			
八 eight	丿	八			
九 nine					

十 ten	一	十		
日 day	丨	冂	日	日
月 moon	丿	刀	月	月
水 water	亅	水	水	水
火 fire	丶	丷	少	火
大 big	一	ナ	大	
小 small	亅	小	小	
上 up	丨	卜	上	
下 down	一	丅	下	

中 middle	丨 冂 口 中
左 left	一 ナ 左 左 左
右 right	一 ナ 才 右 右
你 you	丿 亻 伫 你 你 你 你
我 I	一 二 手 手 我 我 我
她 she	乀 女 女 如 如 她
他 he	丿 亻 仃 伷 他
它 it	丶 宀 宀 它 它

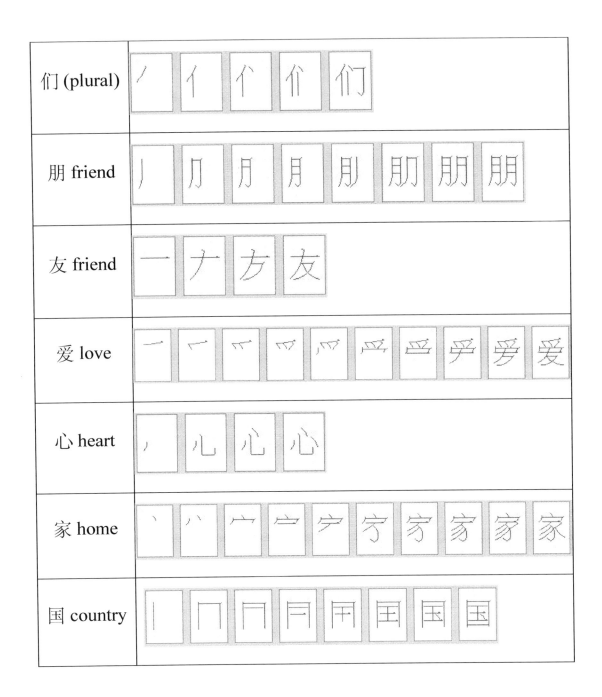

Well-done! BOOK 2 is finished!

Step by Step: mànmàn lái / yí bù yí bù lái 慢慢来 / 一步一步来

Other books in the series by Vivienne Zhang:

Modern Chinese (BOOK 1)

– Learn Chinese in a Simple and Successful Way – Series BOOK 1, 2, 3, 4

Modern Chinese (BOOK 3)

– Learn Chinese in a Simple and Successful Way – Series BOOK 1, 2, 3, 4

Modern Chinese (BOOK 4)

– Learn Chinese in a Simple and Successful Way – Series BOOK 1, 2, 3, 4

Made in the USA
Lexington, KY
26 October 2015